P9-DOA-671

JUSTIN TIMBERLAKE

FAMOUS ENTERTAINER

Peachtree

KATIE LAJINESS

Big Buddy Books

An Imprint of Abdo Publishing
abdopublishing.com

BIG
BUDDY **POP** BIOGRAPHIES

abdopublishing.com

Published by Abdo Publishing, a division of ABDO, PO Box 398166, Minneapolis, Minnesota 55439.
Copyright © 2016 by Abdo Consulting Group, Inc. International copyrights reserved in all countries.
No part of this book may be reproduced in any form without written permission from the publisher.
Big Buddy Books™ is a trademark and logo of Abdo Publishing.

Printed in the United States of America, North Mankato, Minnesota.
102015
012016

THIS BOOK CONTAINS
RECYCLED MATERIALS

Cover Photo: Dan Steinberg/Invision/AP.
Interior Photos: © Mario Anzuoni/Reuters/Corbis (p. 19); Associated Press (pp. 13, 15, 23, 25, 27, 29);
    Robyn Beck/AFP/Getty Images (p. 17); Christie Goodwin/Getty Images (p. 5); Dave Hogan/
    Getty Images (p. 9); Brian Killian/Getty Images (p. 21); KMazur/Getty Images (p. 13); Mike Prior/
    Getty Images (p. 11); © Scripps/Splash News/Corbis (p. 9).

Coordinating Series Editor: Tamara L. Britton
Contributing Editor: Marcia Zappa
Graphic Design: Jenny Christensen

Library of Congress Cataloging-in-Publication Data

Lajiness, Katie, author.
  Justin Timberlake / Katie Lajiness.
      pages cm. -- (Big buddy pop biographies)
   ISBN 978-1-68078-061-1
1. Timberlake, Justin, 1981---Juvenile literature. 2. Singers--United States--Biography--Juvenile litera-
ture. I. Title.
  ML3930.T58L35 2016
  782.42164092--dc23
  [B]
                              2015033044

CONTENTS

ROCK-STAR ACTOR

Justin Timberlake is a talented singer and actor. He was first known as a teen music star. He has grown into one of today's most popular **entertainers**. Justin has fans around the world!

SNAPSHOT

NAME:
Justin Randall Timberlake

BIRTHDAY:
January 31, 1981

BIRTHPLACE:
Memphis, Tennessee

POPULAR ALBUMS:
No Strings Attached, Justified, The 20/20 Experience Part I and II

MAJOR APPEARANCES:
iHeartRadio Music Awards, *Saturday Night Live, The Social Network*

FAMILY TIES

Justin Randall Timberlake was born in Memphis, Tennessee, on January 31, 1981. His father is Randall Timberlake and his mother is Lynn Harless.

When Justin was five years old, his parents decided to separate. He has a stepmother named Lisa and a stepfather named Paul. Growing up, Justin lived with his mother and stepfather.

WHERE IN THE WORLD?

DID YOU KNOW

On *Star Search*, Justin sang country music! He sang Alan Jackson's "Love's Got a Hold on You."

STARTING OUT

Justin began **performing** at a young age. In 1992, he appeared on a television talent show called *Star Search*. In 1993, Justin got a **role** on *The All New Mickey Mouse Club*. On the show, he sang, danced, and acted for a live **audience**.

At 14 years old, Justin was in the Memphis Commercial Appeal Spelling Bee.

In 2000, famous singer Britney Spears and Justin were still close years after they were both Mouseketeers.

BOY BAND

In 1995, Justin helped form a boy band called *NSYNC. In 1998, the group **released** its first album, *NSYNC*.

The band's second album came out in 2000. *No Strings Attached* sold about 1 million copies the first day. Fans were crazy about *NSYNC's music!

DID YOU KNOW ?

In 2000, "Bye Bye Bye" reached number four on the Billboard Hot 100 Chart!

(Left to right) Chris Kirkpatrick, Joey Fatone, Lance Bass, Justin, and JC Chasez made up the band *NSYNC.

DID YOU KNOW

Justified sold more than 8 million copies!

SOLO STAR

Even with *NSYNC's success, Justin wanted to go **solo**. In 2002, he **released** *Justified*. Justin helped write every song on the album. His hard work paid off. In 2004, Justin won two **Grammy Awards** for *Justified*!

In 2003, Justin and singer Christina Aguilera (above) traveled together during their world tour.

13

Justin **released** a second album in 2006. It **debuted** at number one on the Billboard 200 Chart! In 2007 and 2008, he won four **Grammy Awards** for that album!

DID YOU KNOW?

Justin's second album sold 684,000 copies in one week.

In 2007, Justin slimed the crowd during the 20th Annual Kids' Choice Awards in Los Angeles, California.

FUNNYMAN

Justin is also very funny. He has been on *Saturday Night Live (SNL)* many times. *SNL* is a late-night television **comedy** show that has won many **Emmy Awards**. Every show features a **host** and a singer. Justin has hosted *SNL* five times.

DID YOU KNOW?
On *SNL*, Justin once played a female backup dancer for Beyoncé!

In 2009, Justin won an Emmy Award for his work on *SNL*.

MOVIE STAR

Justin is also an actor. In 2007, he was a voice actor in *Shrek the Third*. In 2010, Justin had a **role** in *The Social Network*. This movie is about Facebook, a popular **social media** site.

In 2012, Justin had a role in *Trouble with the Curve*. He played a former baseball player who becomes a successful scout.

In 2012, actress Amy Adams and Justin attended the premiere of *Trouble with the Curve*.

THE 20/20 EXPERIENCE

In 2013, Justin returned to music. He **released** *The 20/20 Experience* in two albums. The first part came out in March 2013. The second was released in September 2013.

DID YOU KNOW ?

Justin wrote many of the songs for both 20/20 Experience albums.

In 2013, Justin sang in New York City, New York, as part of his world tour.

MAKING MUSIC

Justin is also a songwriter and music **producer**. In 2007, he wrote and sang with **rapper** 50 Cent for "Ayo Technology." The next year, Justin worked with Madonna on "4 Minutes." In 2013, he teamed up with Beyoncé on "Rocket."

In 2008, Justin and Madonna sang together at the Roseland Ballroom in New York City.

OFF THE STAGE

Justin leads a very busy life! He married actress Jessica Biel in Italy on October 19, 2012. During their free time, they enjoy traveling together. The couple spends a lot of time in Los Angeles, California, and New York City, New York.

Justin is a very giving person. He has worked with many benefits such as Keep a Child Alive and Hope for Haiti.

Justin and Jessica attend many events together. In 2012, they attended a benefit for the Metropolitan Museum of Art in New York City.

Justin works with many different businesses. In 2005, he started the William Rast clothing line with his friend Trace Ayala. Justin owns part of Ful, a company that makes many kinds of bags.

Justin also owns part of Mirimichi Green. This company works with golf courses to care for their grasses without harming the earth.

Justin is a basketball fan! He owns part of the Memphis Grizzlies *(right)*, a basketball team in Memphis.

BUZZ

DID YOU KNOW?
In 2013, Justin Timberlake first met President Barack Obama.

In 2015, Justin spent time out of the spotlight. In April, he and Jessica welcomed a son named Silas Randall Timberlake.

Justin won the Innovator **Award** at the 2015 iHeartRadio Music Awards. He was honored for his work in music, movies, and fashion.

Justin continues to find success. His fans are excited to see what he does next!

In 2015, Jimmy Fallon *(left)* and Justin appeared on the *Saturday Night Live 40th Anniversary Special.*

GLOSSARY

audience (AW-dee-uhns) a group of people that listens to or watches a show.

award something that is given in recognition of good work or a good act.

comedy a funny story.

debut (DAY-byoo) to make a first appearance.

Emmy Award any of the awards given each year by the Academy of Television Arts and Sciences. Emmy Awards honor the year's best accomplishments in television.

entertainer a person who performs for public entertainment.

Grammy Awards any of the awards given each year by the National Academy of Recording Arts and Sciences. Grammy Awards honor the year's best accomplishments in music.

host to serve as a host. A person who entertains guests.

perform to do something in front of an audience.

producer a person who oversees the making of a movie, a play, an album, or a radio or television show.

rapper someone who raps. To rap is to speak the words of a song to a beat.

release to make available to the public.

role a part an actor plays.

social media a form of communication on the Internet where people can share information, messages, and videos. It may include blogs and online groups.

solo a performance by a single person.

WEBSITES

To learn more about Pop Biographies, visit **booklinks.abdopublishing.com**. These links are routinely monitored and updated to provide the most current information available.

INDEX

J B TIMBERLAKE
Lajiness, Katie,
Justin Timberlake /
R2003646342 PTREE

Atlanta-Fulton Public Library